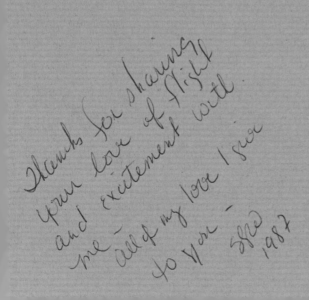

Thanks for sharing
your love of flight
and excitement with
me – all of my love I give
to you – Sara
1987

**Dedicated to the families and friends
of those who serve on the cutting edge.**

Published by Thomasson-Grant, Inc., Frank L. Thomasson and John F. Grant, Directors
Designed by Marilyn F. Appleby
Compiled and edited by Carolyn M. Clark
Photographs and introduction copyright © 1986 by C.J. Heatley III. All rights reserved.
Foreword copyright © 1986 by Senator Jake Garn. All rights reserved.
Illustrations courtesy of Pilot Press.
A-3 illustration courtesy of Arnoldo Mondadori Editore, S.p.A., Milano,
and The Military Press, distributed by Crown Publishers, 1983.
This book, or any portions thereof, may not be reproduced in any form
without written permission of the publisher, Thomasson-Grant, Inc.
Photography and introduction may not be reproduced without permission of C.J. Heatley III.
Foreword may not be reproduced without permission of Jake Garn.
Library of Congress catalog number 85-052216
ISBN 0-934738-17-3
Printed and bound in Japan by Dai Nippon Printing Co., Ltd.
Any inquiries should be directed to the publisher, Thomasson-Grant, Inc.,
505 Faulconer Drive, Suite 1C, Charlottesville, Virginia 22901, telephone (804) 977-1780.

THOMASSON, GRANT & HOWELL

THE CUTTING EDGE

PHOTOGRAPHY AND INTRODUCTION BY C.J. HEATLEY III

FOREWORD BY SENATOR JAKE GARN

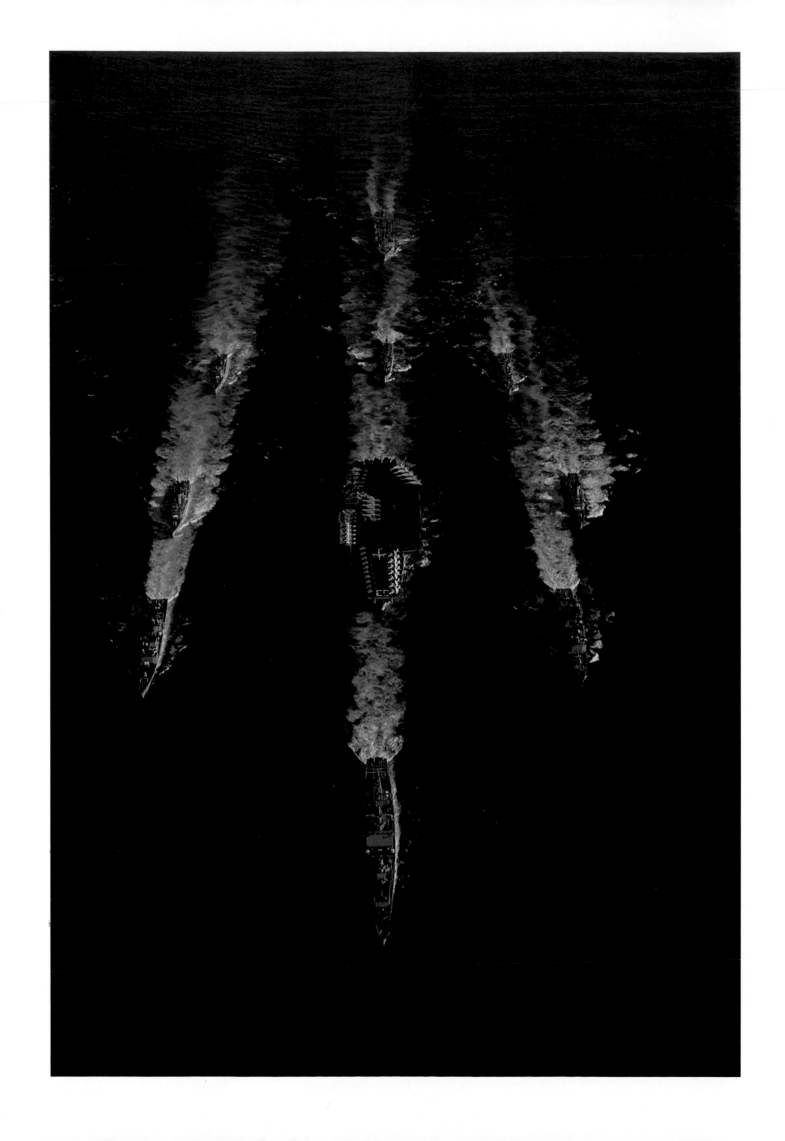

It's difficult for me to describe how proud I am that I wore Navy wings of gold. I never knew a naval aviator who wasn't proud of that fact and who didn't have strong feelings of patriotism. Aviators and the rest of the carrier task group have taken on an important job—protecting the people of the United States and preserving their freedom.

When you have an earth that is 70% water, in any war situation, control of the seas is absolutely critical. We were losing the war against Germany as long as they controlled the North Atlantic. Normandy and D-Day were major turning events, but our success began when we took control of the North Atlantic and got supplies and troops to Europe without devastation. There are also narrow choke points in the world, like the Strait of Gibraltar, that give an advantage to whoever controls them. No matter what we can do on land or in the air, control of sea lanes and choke points will always be important.

In the early days we could control the sea lanes with battle ships and cruisers. When air power developed, it became apparent that the combination of sea and air power would result in a stronger defense. The best use of military power is as a deterrent, and the carrier task force is an incredible projection of power. It has been proven over and over again in peacetime that the carrier task group, by its very presence in a troubled area, can effectively maintain that peace.

This year is the 75th Anniversary of Naval Aviation. Today's carriers are very different from the ones which we had in the 1950s. The computer has revolutionized naval warfare capability in many ways—fire control, navigation, target acquisition, missiles, all kinds of electronic systems. When I was a young midshipman, we spent so much time sitting with our slide rules, looking at the radar, and plotting. Computers changed that. Now when I go aboard a carrier or into its Combat Information Center and look at the incredible amount of information readily available to the captain of a ship or the commander of the air wing, I am amazed. Still, my basic observations about the Navy hold true whether it is the 25th anniversary or the 175th. The technology has changed, but the people haven't. My major thoughts are of the elite group who have served, and the opportunity I have had in my life to work with the best of the best.

Naval aviators are a very select group of people. Look at those who apply to be aviators compared to those who are accepted, and then look at the weeding out process through flight training programs. There aren't any draftees out there on those carriers flying jets. Those men are there because they are willing to take risks to fly for their country.

The pilots, like the astronauts, are the ones who get all the credit, but there is a cast of thousands who backs them up. All those people, the entire carrier task group, are never recognized enough. They are an incredibly dedicated group of human beings who give a lot of themselves. I am pleased that the 75th Anniversary of Naval Aviation gives me the occasion to praise them.

—Senator Jake Garn
May 1986

Morning launches are the best. The dawn patrol. Most of your shipmates are still asleep, and there you are, helmet in hand, walking out to your jet, half a world away from home. The sun glows on one horizon, the stars fade on the other. In an hour the flight deck will churn with activity. Jet engines will roar, catapults scream and hiss, exhaust gases and the smell of jet fuel will taint the air, an unbelievable commotion. Now it's quiet, and the sky is crisp and clear. There's nothing but ocean in every direction.

You get the preflight out of the way and start to think about flying, because flying is what you love to do. There's something about strapping on 50,000 pounds of fire-breathing hardware, roaring off into the heavens and defying the laws of nature. You can't help but marvel at the power and lethality that your country has entrusted to you. One forward motion from your gloved hand kicks in the afterburners, and soon you are outracing your own sound. Faster than a .45 caliber bullet, you can go straight up or straight down. You are a naval aviator, and you are in complete control. It's not often that reality exceeds your dreams. But it did for me.

Everybody plays army when they are kids, but even while I was hiding in the bushes with my toy rifle, I knew I wanted to fly. The old war flicks affected me most—John Wayne, William Holden, Gary Cooper. They made flying seem so glorious. Besides, the soldiers sloshing around in the mud seemed to have so much awe and respect for the guys who flew; they always looked for the "fly-boys" to save them. I didn't want to be in a foxhole with a rifle. I wanted to be the hero with a silk scarf and leather flight jacket.

On television there were World War II documentaries like "Twentieth Century" and "Victory at Sea." I watched our B-17s get jumped by Messerschmidts over Germany and scream for fighter cover. In the Pacific, when our torpedo planes and bombers were attacked by Japanese Zeroes, they too screamed for fighter cover. I wanted to be the guy they were screaming for. I wanted to shoot down Zeroes and Me-109s. When Winston Churchill said, "Never have so many owed so much to so few," he was talking about fighter pilots.

Whether I'd ever fly or not was one thing, but for some reason there was never any doubt about serving in the military. John Wayne may have planted the seed, but I had uncles in the "real" Army, Navy, and Air Force. They fascinated me with stories whenever they'd stop by on leave and sent me their unit patches for my collection. Maybe it was my father's disqualification from a Naval Aviation Cadet program soon after I was born in Pensacola, Florida. I'm not sure what sealed my fate, but I've always looked forward to serving my country in the military.

My youngest brother was influenced by many of the same things and is presently a Navy helicopter pilot. Naturally the "rotor head/jet jockey" rivalry developed in my family, just as it has in the military. If it's not Air Force versus Navy, it's jets versus props, or attack versus fighters, or "air dales" versus "ground pounders." Even between the light attack and medium attack communities there is a lot of ribbing. All pilots are very parochial about their aircraft and always have been. They think theirs is the best and that their mission is the most important. It's a healthy competition, the nature of pilots since the second airplane was built.

I started my freshman year at college feeling pretty guilty that some of my high school buddies were already in Vietnam. Flying military jets required a college degree, but I hadn't even decided who to fly for—the Army, Navy, Air Force, or Marines? I figured if the military is our country's "sword of freedom," then the Navy and Marine Corps would certainly be at the tip of that sword. I liked that. But this was the late-'60s; I was young, and long hair was in. The Navy's somewhat looser haircut standards suddenly appealed to me. Besides, by that time flying was no longer a childhood fantasy. I thought maybe I could fly from carriers, out there in harm's way, on the cutting edge. Navy ROTC at the University of Missouri was my ticket back to Pensacola and flight school.

Becoming a Navy pilot is one of those things that seems impossible. Civilians who marvel at the Blue Angels and other jets in military air shows think, "I could never do that." They don't realize that most of us said the same thing. It's a long learning process, almost two years before you're finally assigned to a deployable squadron, but it's one day at a time. You don't need an aeronautical engineering degree; mine is in journalism. The Navy teaches you everything you need to know. Most aviators will admit however, that had we studied as hard in college as we did to earn our wings, we could have all gotten PhDs. After I finished training, I realized that anybody who really wants those "wings of gold" could earn them. It all boils down to how badly you want it.

And it was worth it. Before I knew it, I was on the USS *Forrestal,* headed out for my first cruise. There was an F-4 Phantom on the flight deck with my name on it. I was never so excited or so proud in my life. The responsibilities that come with being a naval officer hadn't sunk in yet. I was just a carefree young fighter pilot, finally doing what I always wanted to do. I didn't really think about the future beyond the next day's flight schedule.

Later on, I became more and more aware of how important the carrier battle group is. We are not only an instrument of national policy, but our presence overseas is actually required by international treaties. On any given day, we could start or stop a war. This is a high speed, high stakes, high risk business. Screwing up can have catastrophic results: from your own "smoking hole in the ground" caused by a moment's inattention, to getting the carrier blown up because you allowed an enemy aircraft or missile to penetrate your defense. You have to be completely prepared, mentally and physically, each and every hop. It's not just your own life that depends on it. For fighter pilots especially, there are no points for second place. In air-to-air combat, you either get the gold or you're dead.

Some guys love to go on cruise, but for others, cruises can be tough. Especially for families with children who are too young to understand. ("How about if I count to 300, Daddy, will you be home then?") Three weeks into a seven month cruise we stopped in Pearl Harbor, and I called home for the first time since departing San Diego. My five-year-old daughter would not talk to me. In fact, she had not spoken to anyone since the day I left. She coped with my absence by becoming mute. Eventually she began to talk again, though for her I no longer existed. She even left the room when my wife tried to read my letters to her.

My son was another story. Adam not only came to the phone, but he had a plan. "Dad," he said in a secretive whisper, "jump off the ship, and swim;" he paused between each word for emphasis, "swim to land, and get a car, and come home, okay, Dad?" What could I say to this four-year-old "man of the house?" My eyes welled with tears. I couldn't answer. I couldn't even swallow. Before I could relax the painful knot in my throat, he dropped his whisper and said in a clear, loud voice, "COME HOME!" As he passed the phone back to my wife, I could hear him say reassuringly, "Don't worry, Mom, he's coming home." There were six months to go.

As you might imagine, family separations are the number one reason servicemen and women leave the Navy. The number and length of cruises are being cut back as a result; but let's face it, the battle group is not much good tied to a pier. Sailors have got to go to sea.

In order to make this hardship more bearable, shore duty follows every tour of sea duty. These tours are approximately three years long for both officer and enlisted and will alternate for an entire career. You're attached to a ship, squadron, or station. Most sea-going outfits are home-ported in the same area where shore billets are available, so sometimes you can stay in the same place for several years, even though you've been transferred to different units two or three times.

TOPGUN is one of those places. Located at NAS Miramar in San Diego, the Navy Fighter Weapons School (nicknamed TOPGUN) simulates the threat in mock air battles and teaches a graduate level course in fighter tactics. The training is so intense and the learning curve is so steep that TOPGUN has become the subject of books and movies. It's the best five weeks of flying a fighter crew will ever have; the lessons learned are invaluable. After TOPGUN graduates arrived in Vietnam, the Navy's kill ratio improved from 2½:1 to 13:1. TOPGUN instructors are the tactical experts in air combat maneuvering (ACM) and maritime air superiority. Like other adversary pilots, when TOPGUN instructors return to the fleet, they not only bring with them a wealth of knowledge, but also the unique perspective of seeing the Navy's front line fighters from the enemy's point of view.

Flying is the thrilling part, but not all of our time is spent in the cockpit. Our average flight time is only about 25 hours per month, and each flight requires around three hours of briefing and debriefing. Then there are self-study, simulators, and lectures. It takes a lot of billets to run a 300 man, twelve aircraft squadron, so every pilot and Naval Flight Officer has a primary duty that doesn't involve flying. Space is at a premium on an aircraft carrier, so we can't have "ground pounders" (nonflying personnel) doing our administrative functions. We would rather be flying, but these other jobs have to be done. Besides, you can't become a leader in the Navy just by being a good pilot; airmanship is only one grade on a fitness report. You have to be as competent a manager as any corporate executive if you plan to move up the pyramid and run an aircraft carrier someday.

Any time a couple of naval aviators get together, the subject of night carrier landings is bound to come up. Is it as hard as everyone says? No. It's harder. We don't want to ruin our image, so we don't talk about it much to outsiders. More pilots lose their wings because of their landing performance than for all the other reasons combined. Day traps are fun. We'd do them for free and can't get enough of them. The same goes for day catapult shots. But turn out the sun, obscure the horizon with a low ceiling and bad visibility; nobody likes that. Throw in a pitching deck and a thunderstorm; it's like practicing bleeding. Many pilots dread landing on a night like that.

One particularly black night, a squadronmate of mine was having difficulty getting aboard. He had so many looks at the pitching deck that he had to be tanked (inflight refueled) twice, along with a couple of other guys who were having the same problems. Finally, everyone, including the tanker, was safely aboard but him. On the ninth pass, he landed fine, but his hook skipped the wires for a bolter. The tenth time he was high and fast all the way, another bolter. Each approach required so much concentration and effort that his strength, along with his chances of getting aboard, deteriorated each time he went around.

While flying downwind to set up for his eleventh pass, thoughts of his wife and son flashed through his mind. He was convinced he'd never see them again because the sea was too rough and too cold for a rescue. He was low, the deck was coming up. The LSO waved him off at the last second, narrowly averting disaster. This was "blue-water ops;" no divert fields to escape the blackness. Somehow, somewhere, he mustered up all his remaining skill and courage, and on that twelfth and final pass, the wire jerked him mercifully to a halt.

The carrier had to remain into the wind and off course for the entire episode. This put the ship "behind PIM" (position of intended movement) and made it predictable for too long. All the tanker fuel was used up, and flight deck operations were delayed nearly an hour. A normal recovery this wasn't, but then again, this was not a normal night.

When the pilot didn't show up in Maintenance Control to fill out the usual postflight paperwork, I went looking for him. I found him in the passageway, half-way to the ready room, unable to take another step. He was slumped against the bulkhead, exhausted, weeping. His flight gear appeared to weigh a ton. As I approached, his helmet dropped from his hand and bounced off the deck. He was wasted, emotionally and physically drained. "I thought that was it, Heater," he said, visibly relieved that a stranger was not witnessing such a sight. "After the eighth or ninth pass, I knew I was dead."

Every tailhooker has his "turn in the barrel" sooner or later. You just have to take a deep breath and try to say, "What doesn't kill you makes you tougher." That particular pilot flew superbly the rest of the cruise and was a great LSO on the next one. Today, he's an instructor teaching young pilots how to land aboard a carrier.

It may be hard to imagine that people stationed together on the same ship could be strangers, but an aircraft carrier is no ordinary ship. We're a floating city with over 5,000 guys aboard. We've got a post office, library, TV and radio stations, convenience stores, laundry, dry cleaners, chapel, you name it. Everything but a bowling alley. It's a large community where you don't often get to visit all the neighborhoods.

I notice it most when I'm taking pictures. After six months on cruise, I still see new faces. Mostly young faces. The average age for the entire air wing and ship's company is 19½ years old. Watching

them launch and recover aircraft and operate this billion dollar national asset (which we call "the boat") is an impressive sight that I've tried to capture on film. It's also a challenge to record the violence, intensity, and emotion of a night carrier landing. A camera is a good way to share these experiences. To fill the void created by six months of separation, I wanted to create a special slide show, a visual diary of the cruise to show our families and friends when we returned. I wanted it to help them understand what each man went through and how important his contributions are to the overall effort.

Both the battle group and the air wing are a team effort; individuals with specialized skills work together as a coordinated unit. In the air wing, each aircraft has its own specialty. The Battle Group Commander positions his submarines and surface ships in a manner that best protects the carrier. The E-2C Hawkeye, with its long-range radar, launches as the eyes of the fleet. An SH-3 helo is always airborne during flight operations for its SAR (Search and Rescue) capability. A swimmer is part of the crew in case someone is blown overboard or parachutes into the sea. The SH-3's real mission is ASW (Anti-submarine Warfare), so when he's not plane guarding, he looks for enemy subs. The S-3 Viking looks for subs too, but with its tremendous range, he's able to operate far from the ship.

Several fighters position themselves around the carrier in a zone defense. Others escort the strike group, while still more top off their tanks and proceed to the target area to establish air superiority. Whoever needs fuel gets it from designated A-6 and A-7 tankers before or after the mission. The EA-6 Prowler jams enemy radars and radio frequencies, while the EA-3 Skywarrior gathers all sorts of intelligence by monitoring the enemy's entire electronic spectrum.

This all sets the stage for the reason there are carriers and carrier battle groups in the first place—power projection. The ability to cross the beach and do battle in the enemy's backyard. Getting bombs, bullets, and rockets on target is the attack community's business. They're the ones that score. That means A-7 Corsairs, A-6 Intruders, and the new F/A-18 Hornets. The rest of us are supporting players, from the largest ship in the battle group to the guy who swabs the deck. We're all part of a twelve ship, 90 aircraft, 8,000 man team where everyone has a job to do, some more glamorous than others, but all vitally important.

Hollywood may have attracted me to the military, but it certainly didn't keep me there. Like many servicemen, I'm often asked, "Why don't you get out?" Higher paying civilian jobs that allow you to go home at night are certainly attractive. But I just don't think home would be the same without the Navy out there on the cutting edge. I have a job with dignity and purpose. I am surrounded by extremely talented and dedicated people. That's what keeps me in. ▰

— C.J. Heatley III

The flight deck is the most chaotic looking and noisy evolution that I've ever heard. There is no margin for error. There are 40 airplanes out there. If they were in the Air Force, they'd be spotted over acres of land, but they are all pinned to a tiny flight deck, and anywhere from 30 to 40 of them are turning up their engines. That's an awful lot of engines turning at one time, and the catapults and arresting gear engines are noisy. Everyone wears ear protection. We still hear everything; it just reduces the decibels so that it doesn't hurt. Some of us wear a two-way communication helmet, so besides all the noise we are inundated with voice calls. The radio in the helmet is used partly for safety, in case we need to stop something from making a mess on the deck.

If you don't launch or land an airplane about every 35 seconds, then the ship is steaming into the wind too long, and we're too predictable. The more efficiently we get airplanes on and off the deck during cyclic operations, the less predictable the battle group. You can only land or launch when the wind blows down the deck, so for about 20 minutes the ship is very vulnerable; it can't jink away from torpedoes. All the seconds add up, and if one squadron is continually late in landing, the recovery is delayed by minutes. If we take too long, the ship may run into shoals or an island, and then instead of going about its business, the ship has to turn around and head back into the wind.

A flight deck officer coordinates launch and recovery of the aircraft and must account to the air boss. To maintain cyclic operations you always have to think two events ahead. It gets to be a long day, 16 hours on your feet on a steel deck. You have to spot the deck before, during, and after the twelve hours of flying, and then you still have administrative duties. There are 5,000 men on board, with a lot of them right up on the flight deck. I enjoy the rapport between officers and junior people on the flight deck, since most of the men up there are enlisted. It's fun to watch them develop. On the flight deck there are a lot of Indians and very few chiefs.

It's a fun job in spatial relations—will that plane fit in that hole, can you upload or download ordnance? I think of it as an integrated orchestra between weapons, air wing maintenance, air crew, and the air department. ◢

—a flight deck officer

There are usually two catapult officers, one on the waist and one on the bow of the flight deck. Between us we alternate launching a plane every 45 seconds. Behind the catapult is a JBD (jet blast deflector), which helps stop the jet blast of air at takeoff. It is about ten feet high and like a steel barn door. When the plane is positioned on the catapult, you signal the pilot to turn up to full power. Then you take a last look at all the panels, see if the flaps on the plane are set right, make sure the pilot's head is back against the seat. The pilot salutes you if all is well; at night he turns on his lights. You take one last look to see that the deck is clear, and then you crouch down and touch the flight deck. From that time until you point two fingers in the direction that the plane will be catapulted, only you or the air boss can stop the plane. When you point those fingers, then—and only then—does the catapult operator push the button. When the plane is being catapulted off, you stay crouched because the wing passing overhead could take your head off, or the jet blast, which is about 200 miles per hour, could blow you in the water.

The catapult works like two large steam bottles. Accumulated pressure is fed into two long cylinders, with pistons attached to a shuttle inside them. When the steam valves open, the steam enters at a rate which determines the plane's air speed. You determine the amount of steam by considering the weight and type of aircraft. Usually you give them ten knots over what they need to get airborne.

The FDO (flight deck officer) sequences the aircraft to the catapults. The catapults have to build up steam, so you don't want to go from a very light plane, like the A-7E with a max takeoff weight of 42,000 pounds, to something very heavy, like the A-3 with a max of 82,000 pounds. Waiting to build up steam wastes time. The FDO also has to figure who has launch priority in order to reach their target time. It's like putting a jigsaw puzzle together in your head. ◢◤

—a catapult officer

Getting airborne is the only phase of carrier aviation that you, as a pilot, have no control over. It is kind of unsettling to depend on the ship to get you airborne, because there is always the chance that it will go wrong. You either fly or get dumped in the water. The initial acceleration is so fast that it feels like you slow down after leaving the deck. You go from zero to 150 knots instantly. At night it takes your brain two or three seconds to settle down after the catstroke; we call it "getting behind the airplane." You can't see if you are flying or not, and your inner ear is totally fooled by the acceleration. Even the instruments lag during the catstroke, so you're launching on procedures and blind faith.

— *an A-6 pilot*

From the pri-fly tower the air boss controls fueling, launch, recovery, and flight patterns of aircraft. I also command the movement of 400 to 500 people, and must be sure that aircraft are fueled and positioned, that cats and arresting gear function, that handling and fire equipment work.

It is unacceptable to be late. In cyclic ops we launch about 20 planes and then position another set. We must ensure that personnel wear proper clothing and protection, and that they stay away from the jet intake suction. Sometimes planes launch and land at the same time. With such close tolerance in the pattern, launching aircraft must stay at 500 feet until they are well clear of the landing pattern. There is a button in pri-fly that we can push to stop the cat from firing, even after the catapult officer gives the signal. There are a lot of decisions to be made in split seconds; you have to think of so many things at the same time, and you are responsible for whatever happens out there. But naval aviators are trained to make instantaneous decisions. It doesn't bother me. ◢

—an air boss

When I became a pilot, I wanted to fly the F-14 because it was the top-of-the-line Navy fighter. The F-14 has missiles that no other plane in the world has—long-range Phoenix missiles—so a lot of our mock fights could be finished more than 30 miles from the airplane. The Phoenix missile weighs 1,000 pounds, and once activated, chases its target until it finds it. The F-14 also carries four Sidewinders, four Sparrows, and guns. The variable sweep wings enable us to set them at 68° to fly fast, or sweep them out to 20° to land slow and stable. When the new F-14D gets more powerful engines, those wings are going to make it the toughest fighter in the world, in any arena—long-range, medium-range, close-range, and dogfight. Nothing will be able to touch it.

The F-14 is easy to sight in a dogfight because of its size, but there are some advantages to being big. You can carry the Phoenix, and you can carry a lot of gas. The F-14 doesn't have to tank to make normal cycle time. Because of its size, the F-14 can carry a camera in its nose and a TV screen in the cockpit. No matter what the radar says, we must have visual identification of the target before we can launch a missile. The TV camera gives me extended-range visual identification, and I can shoot first.

When bombers make a surgical strike, the fighters act as their cover. On cruise, we are usually on CAP (combat air patrol), acting in a defensive role. Since the enemy can launch cruise missiles from a couple hundred miles out, we need to be out there too, ready to shoot their platform down before they can fire. We are like a zone defense in football or basketball, protecting against intruders. ◢

—an F-14 pilot

The EA-6B is a modified A-6; instead of two men crews, we have four. The canopies are actually gold plated, because back when the EA-6B first came out, they worried about the effects of electronic radiation on the crew. There aren't any. But if you see an EA-6B in the sunlight, the canopy just gleams gold.

We practice electronic warfare by denying the enemy use of their radar. We decide which aircraft are threats and which are friendly, and then the transmitters in our external pods jam the highest threat radar systems. If we can jam their radars, then they can't detect or track our planes. When we're up against early warning radar, which has lower frequency and longer range, it is easier to jam. In that case, the closer we fly to the aircraft that we are protecting, the better. The enemy uses airborne intercept radar when they want to lock up on the target and give strike aircraft a firing solution. Then, the situation is more critical.

I like the EA-6B because you are involved in everyone else's mission. We can pass information to the E-2 or pass radar signals to the ASW (antisubmarine warfare aircraft). We fly all the mission scenarios—it's kind of a warfare specialty, playing in everybody else's game.

We usually work closely with the S-3. The S-3 provides anti-submarine outer-zone offense capability. It carries torpedoes, depth bombs, harpoon missiles, rockets, conventional bombs, and can accoustically measure if an attack is valid. It usually flies double or triple cycles because it carries lots of fuel. The S-3 has flown up to 1,000 miles from the carrier to prosecute a contact, which is why the E-2C often uses them to investigate or assist in targeting surface contacts. With their radio relay pod, they can communicate what they see to all units of the battle force. With FLIR (forward looking infrared) they can classify targets at night. The S-3 is a safe plane because it lands at a slower speed. It is the only plane that can land and launch on the carrier in a tail wind. ◢◤

—an EA-6B pilot

Only a few completely assembled bombs and missiles are in the ready-service lockers. Components of the ordnance have to be broken out of storage areas before assembling; until then it is all kept separate. We usually use the mess decks as work space; sometimes we assemble during the night. Then there are special bomb elevators that give direct access from the magazine to the flight deck. On the flight deck, bombs and missiles are kept on the starboard side of the island, what they call the "bomb farm," prior to being loaded on the aircraft. Before the planes taxi to the cat, you check to be sure their ordnance is correct. Right before they take off, you arm it. If a plane still has ordnance on when it lands, ordnance personnel safe the missiles as soon as the plane taxies clear of the landing area. You have to remember that if it weren't for the ordnance, we wouldn't be out on cruise.

— *an ordnance officer*

When the A-7 was developed in the mid-'60s, the objective was to deliver more bombs further. They didn't necessarily have a more accurate delivery system. That was improved, and now the A-7E is very accurate.

With the A-7 you need multiple plane flights to defend against enemy missiles, guns, electronic warfare. We learn how to fly in formations to protect ourselves; at night in flights of two or more, and in the day, four or more. We usually fly light attack missions, bombing an assigned target. Sometimes we fly close air support, which is mostly a Marine mission, bombing close to our own troops to drive back opposing forces. The A-7 has less than all-weather strike capability, because so much of what the pilot does is visual. In bad weather, the pilot is too busy making flight decisions at low altitudes and in adverse conditions to come up with a weapons delivery tactic.

We practice dive bombing patterns most often. We come in at a 45° angle when there is small arms fire. In a more permissive environment, we come in at 10° or 30°, which is shallower and more accurate. To make a clandestine low approach, you fly in low, drop your bomb, and then pop up high, flying almost straight up. The A-7 doesn't have much excess thrust, so it is vulnerable when it pops up.

You seldom fly an A-7 without a flight leader or section leader flying near you, so there is a lot of competition within the squadron because you can observe the other planes so closely. But I like flying a single person plane. You get to make all the decisions—flight planning, navigation, weapons delivery, landing, and takeoff. ◢

—an A-7 pilot

Everybody talks about the E-2 dome. People tease us about how funny it looks, call it a frisbee, but I say beauty is in the eye of the beholder. The dome is neutral in takeoff or flight; it provides as much lift as parasitic drag. In a three million cubic mile area, nothing moves on land, air, or water without our knowledge. We have a number of radios—UHF, HF, data link—and passive receivers that give off no RF energy. We share coded data link on a two-way communication with the Tomcat, and provide one-way information to light and medium attack planes. We are also the link to all surface craft, reporting directly to Alpha Bravo, the battle group coordinator. The entire airwing is structured around mutual support, and the E-2 is the integrator. We are the eyes of the fleet.

— *an E-2C pilot*

Fighter pilots always want to dogfight. That's the whole reason they became fighter pilots. It's man and machine against man and machine. He's capable; you're capable. Hopefully you are on the offensive, trying to take a shot, but you also have to keep him from getting a bead on you. You can't be predictable or you'll get bagged.

When you train, you start off fighting similar planes, one-versus-one at cospeed and co-altitude. Just learning the basics takes over nine hours of academic instruction and 30 hours of reading and research. Then you fight dissimilar planes, called bogeys, then try more exotic scenarios, like not knowing the number or position of the planes as the fight begins.

Dogfighting has changed since World War II. With new technology, you no longer have to saddle up at the enemy's six o'clock, you can shoot head-on as you are closing. Basically, you can shoot anyone you can see. In a dogfight you pull hard and fast to lock up on the radar and get a tone on your heat-seeking missile. Either that, or you get a radar lock and shoot your Sparrow. When you choose missiles, you go strictly by range, but it's always nice to get rid of the Sparrow first, because it weighs more. If the enemy gets through your Sparrow and Sidewinder envelope, then you use your guns. But that's close, predictable, and dangerous.

As any pilot has been taught since day one, the key to success in a dogfight is keeping sight of who you're flying against. There is a saying, "lose sight, lose the fight." It isn't like the old days with biplanes a hundred feet apart. We have missiles that shoot beyond ten miles. Even close-in missiles are considered close at one to four miles. At four miles an airplane is just a speck, and you have to be able to maneuver against him, or that speck is going to get the advantage, get his nose on, and kill you. ◢

—an F-14 pilot

When someone shoots a heat-seeking missile at you, you send off a flare. Flares are made of magnesium, which burns hotter than jet exhaust, so the missile seeks the flare instead of you. Then you come out of afterburner, which also gives you less heat, and you turn away hard, probably about six and a half Gs. If you are ready for the turn, it isn't bad. Pulling Gs really tires you out, but your body gets more used to it the more you fly. The oxygen mask presses on your nose; your lungs and heart press on your diaphragm, and your back and butt are crushed in the seat. I literally weigh 1,300 pounds when I'm pulling six and a half Gs. As the blood leaves your head, you see dots, and then gray, and then tunnel vision, because there is an inadequate blood supply feeding your eyes. When you feel the force coming, you practice the grunt, or M-1 maneuver, by tensing your legs and torso, to hold the blood in your head so you don't black out. If you do a good M-1, you can lessen the effects of the forces by about one G.

— an F-14 pilot

Sunballs are circular rainbows around the sun; you only see them when you are between the sun and the clouds. Sometimes, you can use them to your advantage in a dog-fight. You try to position yourself between the sun and your opponent, so that he's directly in front of the circle of the sunball. Then you fly the sunball over to him. He can't look straight into the sun and therefore can't see you. If he did shoot a heat-seeking missile at you, it would be drawn to the sun instead of your plane.

— *an F-14 pilot*

The FA-18 is an air-to-air and air-to-ground strike-fighter that was designed to replace aging F-4S fighters and A-7E attack aircraft. Since day one, it was built from the ground up for what we call "big R little m"— total reliability and very little routine maintenance. So far, the FA-18 has been more reliable than any other tactical plane. To pilots, this means the FA-18 is always up and ready to fly.

When they designed the FA-18, they put a lot of proven advanced technology in it. The FA-18 is constructed with composite materials—plastics—so it is strong and lightweight, capable of carrying a lot of ordnance. The weapons in our arsenal include Sparrow and Sidewinder air-to-air missiles, the M-61 gattling gun, and virtually every air-to-ground weapon in the Navy inventory. The radar has numerous modes that can track multiple airborne targets, fire missiles, navigate, and deliver air-to-ground weapons with pinpoint accuracy. And with our high-tech GE TF-404 engines, the FA-18 has more thrust-to-weight for acceleration and maneuvering performance than any other tactical carrier jet. The net result of all this technology is a highly capable combat aircraft that can go anywhere and do everything well.

Since the FA-18 is a single-seat aircraft, I have to do everything myself. So the stick, throttles, and cockpit switches that interface with onboard systems and computers were all designed to optimize pilot operation. In the words of the computer world, the FA-18 is "user friendly." For example, say that I'm navigating to a target with my radar ready, and I see an airplane that I have to turn and fight. Without taking my hands off the stick and throttle, I can switch from navigate to fighter mode, track, and shoot.

A single-seat aircraft also lessens the overcrowding problem on a carrier. One pilot means one less stateroom, less dirty laundry. That's very significant when there are two squadrons of FA-18s aboard the carrier.

Of course it's a real challenge to train for both strike and fighter missions, but we love it. We say there are only two types of pilots, those who fly the FA-18 and those who wish they did. ◢◣

—an FA-18 pilot

A shock wave forms on the aircraft when it reaches supersonic speeds. From the front of the plane, the shock wave appears as a circle, but from the back and sides, it looks like very sharp spikes coming off the plane. It is a rare and spectacular sight, only visible in humid weather. Usually the planes are up too high when supersonic for a visible vapor wave, and since you can't fly supersonic around populations, very few people have caught it stateside.

When you go supersonic, you don't feel a thing. It's not the Chuck Yeager story anymore. Planes that are designed to go supersonic go right through "the number" without a blink. The airplane is as comfortable to fly at landing speeds as it is supersonic. Things just happen faster.

— an F-14 pilot

flew for years as a fleet fighter pilot. As a TOPGUN instructor I became the bogey (bad guy) in the A-4. We use A-4s and F-5s to simulate bogeys because they are small, maneuverable, and hard to see, with a good thrust-to-weight ratio. And it's good for the guys to fight against dissimilar aircraft. Every time we fly against a TOPGUN class, we tell the students what threat tactics the bogeys will simulate. So if we say we're going to simulate two Soviet MiG-21s that day, we present the formation scenario that we taught them for that particular hop.

There are numerous hours of ground school at TOPGUN. Every instructor has a lecture, something to do with tactics or air combat training. Then we fly against the class. Every day that we act as a bad guy, we have to evaluate the good guy's tactics—what might work better or where he went wrong, like in guns defense, or some area where he could fly his airplane more efficiently. You point those things out in debrief, what they did good and what needs improvement, so that when it's over, they can go back and teach other aircrew in their squadron.

It's difficult to take the ego out of the fight and to remember that you are the teacher. It's like being a sparring partner—you are expected to lose sometimes so that he can improve. But you learn a lot by being the bad guy. I see fighters make the same mistakes I used to make, and I think, I don't want to do that again. Or if they do something really great, it reinforces good tactics, and I think, I've got to remember that trick when I get back to the fleet. An instructor gets a very good perspective of what the enemy can and can't do, whereas an aircrew can only guess when they're in the fighter. You see what works, what doesn't work, and what the enemy's viewpoint is.

—a TOPGUN instructor

When a squadron returns from a six-month deployment, you have turn-around time to train for the next cruise. During that period of about twelve months, if you are one of the aircrew chosen by your commanding officer, you attend the Navy Fighter Weapons School (TOPGUN) as a student. It is very competitive; to be selected you need to have been on at least one cruise so that you know how to fight your airplane and employ its weapons systems. But you can't just be a good pilot or radar intercept officer; they also judge your performance as an officer and consider whether you would be a good teacher when you complete the five-week course and return to the squadron.

TOPGUN begins with pure academics. The presentations have all been critiqued by other instructors so that the material is flawless and their delivery is perfect. After a few days of full-time lectures, we attend half-day lectures and fly in the afternoon, and then fewer lectures, with flying twice a day.

At TOPGUN you can achieve a point of aviation proficiency that is impossible to acquire anywhere else. Outside of wartime, it is the toughest environment you can fly, and you can concentrate on mastering the subleties of flying. We do learn some specifics, like facts about air-to-air weapons of other countries, that you could get by reading. But you would never have the time to sift through all that material. The lectures you hear in a couple hours have taken hundreds of hours to research and prepare. So TOPGUN students receive all this great information while devoting almost 100 percent to flying.

When we return to our squadrons, the idea is to give the same lectures we heard at TOPGUN. But you have to lay low for awhile. You can't go back and say, listen to me, I just went to TOPGUN, or the guys in the squadron will resent you. The information begins to come out in debriefs, when you answer questions about strategy or explain why certain things are done. A lot more surfaces before fighter derby competition, when the squadron relies on their TOPGUN graduates to improve their skills so that they can win. ◢

—a TOPGUN student

TOPGUN instructors, like fleet squadron pilots, practice shooting at a 7 × 40 nylon banner that is attached to a support plane by a 2,500 foot cable. The banner is much smaller than an aircraft, so shooting at it is a good way to practice air-to-air gunnery using the gunsight. All of the bullets are marked with wet, sticky paint—red, blue, black, yellow, green—and each pilot has an assigned color. That way, when the exercise is over, we can count the different colored marks on the banner and see who hit it the most.

— *a TOPGUN instructor*

Refueling is difficult to learn. Even though there are lights on the basket to help, it's always tricky at night. Still, it's just like learning to ride a bicycle, once you've done it, it seems easy. It isn't the type of task that you say to yourself, oh my god, I've got to tank today. It's just something you do before going on a mission, grab a couple thousand pounds of fuel from the tanker, and you're on the way. They are phasing out the A-3 as a tanker, but they used to use it because it carried so much gas. Now there are A-6s and A-7s dedicated as tankers on every launch. The tankers can give 400 to 500 pounds of fuel a minute, so refueling takes eight to ten minutes from joinup to breakaway. They can carry up to 16,000 pounds of fuel, but they always save extra gas for the recovery, in case anybody in that launch has trouble landing and needs to refuel. The tankers are always the last guys to land.

As we fly a mission, we continually calculate our remaining fuel supply. You take off with enough fuel to meet cycle time, which is usually one plus 45 (an hour and 45 minutes). If, through miscalculation, you run out of gas and return to the carrier, they have to clear the deck because planes are parked in the landing area, and then you mess up the rhythm of cyclic operations. Usually running out of gas isn't a problem, but with tactical planes, you have to think about afterburner. It nearly doubles the thrust of the engine, but it also quadruples fuel consumption—that's why you have to be prudent. If you aren't, you could be out of fuel in a very short time. You have to see afterburner to believe the power, it looks like rocket flames coming out the exhaust.

Some pilots draw up a fuel ladder. Then they can glance at it every few minutes to see if they have as much fuel as they'd like to have at that point in the cycle. The F-14 has five stages of afterburner, called zones. They aren't marked on the throttle, you can just feel which zone you are in, and you modulate afterburner for more or less thrust, as the mission requires. The higher the zone, the more fuel you use. You hope to have extra fuel on every hop, a "combat package" to light burner for aerobatics, dogfights, or supersonic flight. Fuel is a weapon, just like any other; you can use it to maneuver and win a fight, or you can use it to run away fast if you have the disadvantage. ◢█

—an F-14 pilot

About 1,500 miles out of port, and anytime in the Mediterranean, you are tracked by the Russians. The long-range bombers—Bears and Badgers—can come out several hundred miles to investigate the carrier, anytime they see the battle group as a threat, or when they want to gather intelligence from electronic signals and radio conversations. Sometimes their satellites have trouble keeping track of us, especially if there is any kind of weather cover. So we play games, called electronic emissions control. Nobody does anything electronic on the air—no radios or radar; the ship is invisible. We can go for days without them sighting us. When they do find us, they might send out a regiment of fighters to practice attacking us, and we practice defending. This can go on day and night. Usually our mission is to escort them, but we are also interested in intelligence and what weapons they carry. As long as we follow the rules of engagement, there aren't any incidents.

It gets your heart beating, because all your training is to find those guys, especially their fighters, and shoot them down. It's as close as you can get to the real thing without having ordnance explode. Like when Mohammed Ali met Joe Frazier before the match, there is all that tension and energy. It's nose-to-nose.

With the bombers it is a more relaxed atmosphere, because we know they won't bomb the carrier, and we can see if they have weapons loaded. We signal each other with hand signals and talk to them on the radio. They speak pretty good English. They ask us what it's like to be on a carrier; we tell them we're there for the dancing girls. It's real informal. Usually they just wave.

Even though it's more relaxed with the bombers, they also try to drag us off on other ships and into the water, and sometimes they shine high intensity white lights on us so we can't see. But everybody is a professional pilot, and if they are able to drag you in the water or cause you to hit a ship, then you deserve it, probably. I don't hold it against them. It's a war game that both sides understand. ◢

—an F-14 pilot

Even though a carrier is enormous, landing an airplane on one is still a game of inches. When you touch down on an aircraft carrier, you've only got 400 feet of runway in front of you before you hit the water. There are four arresting wires 45 feet apart; your target is wire number three. If you are a foot high, you can bolter, miss all the wires. If you are low, you can catch early wires, or worse yet, crash into the ship. Sometimes you can get a spitting wire, one that catches the tailhook and then bounces off.

As the LSO (landing signal officer), I stand on the back of the ship. The LSO has a radio just in case the pilot needs assistance, but "in case" usually doesn't happen. I rate their passes with one of four grades. "Okay" is a green pass. That's an excellent pass or one with very timely and precise corrections for minor deviations. A "fair" pass is not as good, but still safe. The next is "no grade," dangerous to yourself, other people, and other planes. A "cut" pass is the worst, so unsafe that it could easily result in a mishap.

The average naval aviator is real good at what he does; he does it for a living, and he's proud of it; therein lies the fraternity. As the LSO, I have to critique the pilots' abilities, what they hold dearest, and they are always defensive. So you have to develop credibility, be consistent, stress the positive. Most pilots have a love/hate relationship with the LSO until it's night or bad weather. Then it's clear that I have the responsibility for saving a life or an airplane. Night is the great equalizer. ◢◣

—*a landing signal officer*

Day landings are fun. We look forward to them, get as many as we can. Work during the daytime is like a ride at the carnival, no anxiety at all. You usually join up over the ship for landings, with all the different types of planes circling at different altitudes. As soon as the deck is cleared, the fighters go down, and then the light-attack planes, and so on. One airplane lands approximately every 45 seconds.

Trapping on a carrier is violent. The seat restraint harness is locked, and when the airplane stops in two seconds, you are thrown totally forward and hang in the straps. You always prepare for a go-around in case the tailhook misses the wire. A jet engine takes three to five seconds to come up to power, so you add 100 percent just as you think you've hit the wire in case you miss all the wires, and have to circle again. Otherwise, you're in the water.

Later we can watch our landings on a videotape that has been recorded by the PLAT (pilot landing aid television). The PLAT uses a combination of two cameras, one mounted on the centerline of the ship, and one manually operated in a glass-enclosed area below the bridge. The LSO can watch the PLAT, but his own eyes are better, because the PLAT is one dimensional and only shows basic trends.

We do our first carrier landing in the training command, in a T-2C Buckeye. That separates the men from the boys pretty early. It is nothing like landing a fighter; the speeds are a lot slower, but it's still an overwhelming experience. Landing on a carrier is a goal in your mind from day one; you've seen movies and pictures and talked to other people about it. Some of the edge is taken off with practice, but it's still hard to anticipate. You go from 150 miles per hour to nothing in two seconds. ◢▰

—*an FA-18 pilot*

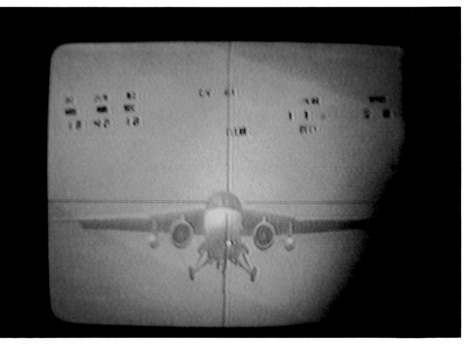

hen you fly blue water operations, there is no place for the airplane to land except on the carrier. If a plane's landing gear is broken, the arresting cable can wrap around it, sluing the airplane to the right where it can crash into people or parked airplanes. If there's an emergency, we land everyone else first and put up the jet blast deflectors to protect the other airplanes. Next, the procedure is to strip all the wires off the flight deck. Then you set up the barricade, which is a bunch of nylon webbing straps that catch the airplane and hold it straight on rollout.

It isn't natural for a pilot to fly an approach when something is in his way. You wouldn't race a car straight into a full parking lot. It's alien to everything normal and comfortable. So you explain to him what he can expect to see. That's a 15 or 18 foot high barricade with straps barring his view of the flight deck, with steel stanchions holding it up and occasionally blocking his view of the meatball.

The only part of the airplane designed to pull it to a stop is the tailhook. So when you land in the straps, they dig into the airplane. Normally a barricade does extensive damage that takes two or three months to repair. This barricade stopped a plane beautifully, and the plane was flying again in two weeks. ◣◣

—a landing signal officer

ight landings are definitely the hardest thing that a naval aviator does. At nighttime there is a lot of anxiety, different degrees for different people, usually varying with the level of experience. If it is nighttime with a moon and a horizon, it isn't so bad. Without a horizon or stars, especially in the rain, it's scary. You haven't seen dark until you're in the middle of the ocean with only a few red lights. You find yourself promising God that you'll be good, and your heart is pounding.

When you get together to land at night, everybody is stacked up; it's called the Marshall Pattern. You start at 5,000 feet and every thousand feet above that is another guy a mile further back, so at 20 miles you are at 5,000 feet, at 21 miles you are at 6,000 feet. The split in miles and in altitude is for safety. Every minute somebody leaves the circle. They tell you your push time, and as you hit that number, you have to be right on altitude. Everyone goes down by that same path.

They did a study in Vietnam, monitoring heartrate, breathing, and some other biological functions. They studied pilots during cat-strokes, trips over to Indian country, refueling, getting missiles shot at them, forming up afterwards, and night landings. The thing that pegged out the needles, that caused the most stress, was the night landings.

The most concern at night is the amount of gas and the weather conditions. If you have a lot of gas, you might be relaxed enough to make a normal approach and land. But if your gas is low, you might get uptight and think, if I miss, I might have to divert to a foreign field, I might have to go tank, I might have to take a barricade. One day you may have a great landing, and then the next day, it's as if snakes are in the cockpit. It often depends on your physiological condition that day, all kinds of intangibles. Everybody has his night in the barrel, making pass after pass. ◢◤

—an A-7 pilot

At night, at three quarters of a mile, the LSO says, "roger ball," meaning he has control of the pass. You listen to him and watch the ball. On the left side of the carrier deck are a vertical and a horizontal row of lights, called the Fresnel lens optical landing system. They fan out into a bar, with an effective focal length of 150 feet. An orange ball of light, called the meatball, is aligned with a row of green lights. If the orange light is above the green lights, you are above glide path. If it is below, you are too low. When the orange is in a straight row with the green, the glide path is perfect. Around the meatball are red lights that are normally off. If they flash, that's a waveoff, meaning it isn't safe to land. There are only ten to twelve seconds from when we enter the groove to when we touch down, so that is all the time they have to wave us off.

— *an S-3 pilot*

I'm what they call a "yellow shirt". When a plane is up and ready to launch, we direct it to the catapult. When it lands, we direct it to the proper place. There are five or six yellow shirts in each of the three fly areas. They try to break us of the habit of walking with the plane; we are supposed to direct it through our territory and then pass it off to the next guy. A good aircraft director doesn't care what type of plane he's directing.

On the flight deck we have a Mickey Mouse (radio), but we use mostly hand signals. You can talk all day with your hands. Every place on the ship has a common sense signal, like if you want to park a plane in the pocket, you just reach around and pat your back pocket.

There is constant danger on the flight deck, so you have to be 100 percent all the time. You can be sucked up, run over, blown over, knocked down. I've had warm jet wash hit me at knee level and blow me through the air ten or twelve feet before I could catch onto something. We always practice safety because you want to come back with the same number of men you left with. To stay sharp we have fire drills every one to three days. There are so many fire hazards: burning metal, toxic fumes, heated-up weapons, exhaust, fuel, electric wires, alpha fires. That's when your clothing or seats catch. Exhaust from an airplane can overtemp something, or fuel on the deck can light and drop down a catapult. Drills teach us how to position ourselves the safest way, and we practice charging the fire, knocking it down, cooling the weapons. A fire that lasts over 40 seconds is big trouble.

Eighteen hours is a long day, but I love it. Practically the only thing there is to do is work, so you don't complain. Nonrated personnel sleep in the "animal coop," with 50 to 100 men in a room. Petty officers are luckier, we stay in rooms with 30 to 40 men. All we have is our bunk, and what we call a "coffin locker," because the lid raises up and down. It's amazing how men can make that one little space look like home.

They try their best to entertain us. About once a month they have boxing or volleyball. Then there's the Gonzo Olympics when you enter the Indian Ocean. Some days they have safety stand down, but we call it "steel beach" because they talk to us about safety for a while, and then everyone just lays around and reads and listens to music on deck.

Of course you're lonely on cruise. All you see is men. You have to harden yourself; I call it "getting in the cruise mode." Once you get in that mode, the days just pass. Half the time you don't know what day it is. ◢◤

—*a petty officer*

The mission of the H-46 is VERTREP (vertical replenishment). We deliver everything from beans and bullets to mayo and movies. Two ships don't have to come alongside; we can replenish from over the horizon. It is a rewarding mission to support the fleet with what they need, when they need it. I also like the camaraderie of detachment life, and in the H-46 the commanding officer is often a lieutenant commander, which gives you an opportunity early in your career to have the responsibility of command. We work closely with the surface force, sustaining the battle group and keeping them flexible. We service Navy ships of all types, as long as they have an 8 x 8 landing area. Unlike the fixed wings, we can land on decks much smaller than a carrier's. But the small boys, the destroyers and frigates, are harder to service in rough seas. They pitch more.

The tandem rotors of the H-46 make us more maneuverable, give us a stable platform for hovering. There are two enlisted men in back. They look down what we call the "hell hole," and when the helo is in position, they say, "I have the load," then, "load is clear, easy up." We try to minimize time by practicing our aim, because time with two ships alongside is always more dangerous.

The load is attached to the H-46 by a cargo hook, from which a pennant is suspended to carry the load in a sling or net. A normal carry is from 1,500 to 6,000 pounds. We can also evacuate 20 plus people in our secondary mission of search and rescue. Sometimes we bring back retrograde, empty bomb cans, repairables. Sometimes we lift an injured crewman on a Stokes litter and carry him to the nearest battle group ship with a doctor. If there is a downed aviator in the water, we wrap a harness around him and lift him.

It is definitely a combat support role, not combat. We do it day and night.

—an H-46 pilot

like being close to the ground in a helicopter. You can fly the machine in any direction; when you move sideways or backwards, or stay still in the air, you really feel that you're defying gravity.

We're the only ones who can fly with the windows open, but flying a helo isn't like driving a car; you don't have any hood or emblem for visual reference. You're smack up front, like a bus driver, and you fly more by looking through the windscreen than by instrument display. We have fewer aids than the fixed wings have to get us on and off the ship. Without electronic glide slope information, we decelerate and stop using only our judgement and brakes. We don't have to land on the angle deck; we could land in a farmer's field if we had to, but unlike a fixed-wing pilot, we know that if there's a problem, we can never jump out or eject.

The SH-3 employs both sonobuoys and active sonar in its antisubmarine role. A sonobuoy is a cylinder that weighs about 30 pounds. A parachute or rotochute drops the sonobuoy in the water. Then it puts out an antenna and a hydrophone, gives off energy, listens to the echoes, and relays that information to the helo. Active sonar is different. We hover at 40 feet and dip it in the water. When you're hovering, you can't tell if you're moving over the water or not. Doppler radar helps you hold the helo steady while dipping the sonar.

It's a challenge to keep track of a moving sub and to match your wits against a submarine CO. We practice antisubmarine warfare against American subs in the battle group, and when we find an enemy sub, we practice tracking it. Submarines have several devices that give false sonar contacts: targets that run off and act like submarines, air bubbles, or noisemakers. They can come to a dead stop, which confuses us, because then, the submarine looks like a false contact. Sometimes they sink, try to make the sonar go through changes in water temperature so that it doesn't work as well.

The best way to shoot a sub is to hover with a sonar contact and drop a torpedo. That way there is no navigation error, you just shoot it and watch it go without worrying about inaccuracies. If the sub is fast, you drop the torpedo ahead of him. ◢◤

—an SH-3H pilot

AIRCRAFT AND CARRIER FACTS

USN designation: F-14A Tomcat
Nickname: Tomcat, Turkey

The F-14 is a twin-engine, two-seat, variable-sweep wing, supersonic fighter. The variable-sweep wing is its most prominent aerodynamic feature. A computer automatically positions the airfoil, even during high-G maneuvers, for aerodynamic efficiency. Other characteristics contributing to the F-14's remarkable performance are a horizontal stabilizer that operates for pitch as well as roll control, twin rudders that give directional control even under the asymmetric load conditions of missile-firing, and a fuselage that forms more than half the total aerodynamic lifting surface.

The F-14 carries the AWG-9 weapons control system, which is capable of simultaneously attacking six different targets, while tracking 18 others. The look-down/shoot-down radar performs against multiple targets, both opening and closing, from all aspects, and at all altitudes. It controls the launching of Tomcat's long-range Phoenix, medium-range Sparrow, and short-range Sidewinder missiles, and the firing of the M-61 cannon.

The aircraft's radar can discern fighter-size targets at more than 100 nautical miles, across a 120 mile-wide scan sector, with high resistance to electronic countermeasures. Looking down, it picks up low-flying targets against surface clutter. A two-way digital data link allows the Tomcat to share information with surface or airborne intercept control. In the nose of the plane, a camera with a 10:1-magnification television sight provides visual target identification at ranges of ten miles and more.

Primary function: attack and destroy multiple airborne targets in all weather conditions and at night
Prime contractor: Grumman Aerospace Corporation
Power plant/manufacturer: two Pratt & Whitney TF30-P-414A turbofan engines
Thrust: 20,000 pounds each engine with afterburner
Dimensions: wingspan 64 feet 1 inch, length 62 feet 9 inches, height 16 feet
Speed: Mach 2+ class
Ceiling: above 50,000 feet
Combat radius: 578 miles
Armament: six Phoenix, four Sparrow, and four Sidewinder missiles; one 20mm MK-61A1 Vulcan cannon
Maximum takeoff weight: 62,260 pounds
Crew: two—pilot, naval flight officer

Photographs: Pages 2-3, viewed from F-14 cockpit; 4-5, 8, 12-13, 16, 17, 20, foreground; 23, 24-25, 28-29, 30, cockpit; 31, 35, viewed from F-14 cockpit; 36, cockpit; 42-43, 44, cockpit; 45, 46, foreground; 50-51, 56-57, viewed from F-14 cockpit; 58, 60, 61, 62, 63, 68, 69, 70-71, foreground; 84-85, being refueled by A-6; 86, being refueled by A-3; 87, being refueled by A-3; 88-89, being refueled by A-3; 90-91, 92, escorting Russian May; 99, escorting Russian Bears; 100-101, 103, 106-107, 110, 112, 113, 114-115, 117, 118, foreground; 119, 120, background; 121, cockpit; 124, foreground; 125, 128-129, 140-141, 142, 150-151, 152.

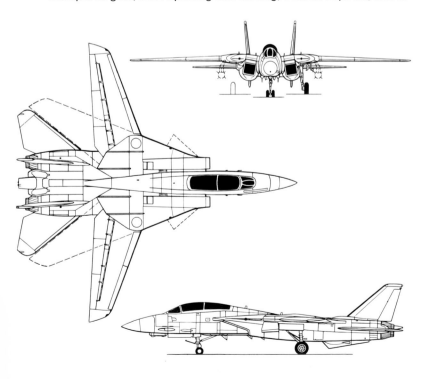

F/A-18

USN designation: F/A-18 Hornet
Nickname: Hornet

The F/A-18 is a multi-mission fighter and attack aircraft designed for use by the U.S. Navy and Marine Corps in the 1980s and 1990s. It replaces Navy A-7s and Navy and Marine Corps F-4s.

A high-performance tactical aircraft, the F/A-18 Hornet can execute fighter, strike, or intercept missions. It is a "fly-by-wire" aircraft, with a central data computer system that handles more than one mission. With interchangeable weapons stations, the F/A-18

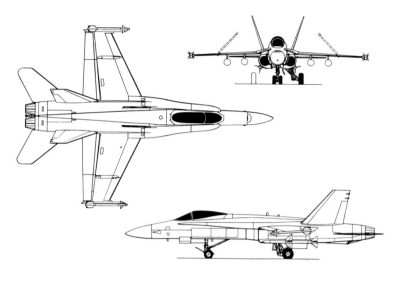

can be tailor-loaded for each operation. The twin-engine aircraft is capable of operating from both aircraft carriers and shore bases.

Primary function: multi-mission fighter and attack aircraft
Prime contractor: Douglas Aircraft Company, McDonnell Douglas Corporation
Power plant/manufacturer: two General Electric F404-GE-400 turbofan engines
Thrust: 16,000 pounds each engine
Dimensions: wingspan 37 feet 6 inches, length 56 feet, height 15 feet 3 inches
Speed: Mach 1.7+
Ceiling: over 50,000 feet
Combat radius: fighter over 400 nautical miles, attack over 550 nautical miles
Armament: one 20mm MK-61 Vulcan cannon, fighter—Sparrow III and Sidewinder missiles; attack—guided and conventional air-to-ground ordnance, FLIR/LDT pods
Maximum takeoff weight: fighter—35,000 pounds, attack—51,900 pounds
Crew: one—pilot

Photographs: Pages 59, 64, cockpit; 65, 66-67, viewed from F-18 cockpit.

A-7

USN designation: A-7 Corsair II
Nickname: Corsair, SLUF

The Corsair II is the U.S. Navy's light attack plane. With the introduction of the A-7E, several innovations improved the Corsair II's weapons delivery capability. A fully integrated avionics package with a microminiaturized digital computer increases weapons delivery accuracy. A head-up display presents continuous solution cues for bombing and navigation on a transparent mirror directly before the pilot's eyes. This enables him to concentrate on his mission without reference to cockpit instruments. With the central digital computer calling the signals and presenting solutions, the pilot can drop, flip, or toss bombs over-the-shoulder at ground targets with great precision.

The computer-directed map navigation system stores maps of selected areas of the earth, covering a million square miles on a single role of 35mm film. Other avionics features include Doppler and forward-looking radar, and an inertial measuring unit.

Primary function: precision air support of front-line troops and tactical zone bombing
Prime contractor: Vought Aeronautics Division of LTV Aerospace Corporation
Power plant/manufacturer: A7-A—Pratt & Whitney TF30-P-6 turbofan engine, A-7B—Pratt & Whitney TF30-P-8 engine, A-7E—Allison TF41-A-2 engine
Thrust: A-7A—11,300 pounds, A-7B—12,200 pounds, A-7E—15,000 pounds
Dimensions: wingspan 38 feet 9 inches, length 46 feet 1 inch, height 16 feet 1 inch
Speed: A-7A/B—Mach .89, A-7E—Mach .92
Range: ferry 2,485 nautical miles (maximum internal and external fuel)
Armament: 15,000 pounds of bombs and rockets, two 20mm cannons, Sidewinder missiles; A-7E—M-61 Vulcan cannon
Maximum takeoff weight: A-7A/B—38,000 pounds, A-7E—42,000 pounds
Crew: one—pilot

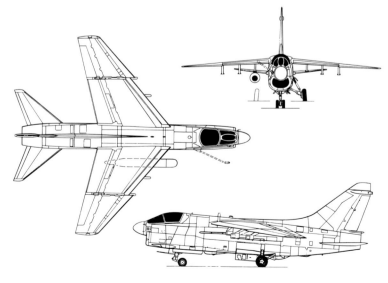

Photographs: Pages 26-27, 37, 46, background; 53, 118, background; 124, background.

A-4

USN designation: A-4 Skyhawk
Nickname: Scooter

The A-4 Skyhawk has proven to be the workhorse of the U.S. Navy's attack squadrons. Designed in 1950-52 as a successor to the reliable, prop-driven Skyraider, the A-4 was approximately half the gross weight proposed by Navy specifications.

A simple, low-cost, lightweight attack and ground-support aircraft, the Skyhawk can also deliver a nuclear weapon. The A-4 has a modified, delta, low-aspect-ratio wing with moderate wing loading. This gives the aircraft excellent low-altitude, high-speed flying capabilities. Skyhawk ordnance includes 20mm guns, rockets, missiles, and a variety of bombs which can be delivered by lay-down, glide, loft, over-the-shoulder, and ground-controlled modes. Ordnance stores are carried externally on pylons and racks under fuselage and wings.

No longer assigned to fleet squadrons, the A-4 is a shore-based plane currently used by the Blue Angels, soon to be replaced by the F/A-18. The primary role of the A-4 is to simulate "bogeys" in air combat training; it also serves the fleet by towing aerial targets. The TA-4 is the last jet a student flies in the training command before he receives his wings.

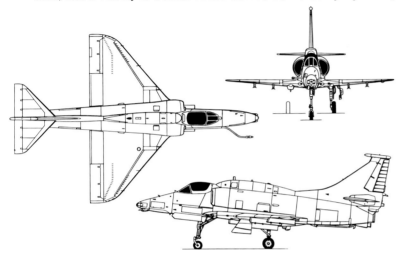

Primary function: adversary simulation and other services for the fleet
Prime contractor: Douglas Aircraft Company
Power plant/manufacturer: A-4B/C—Pratt & Whitney J65-W-16A engine, A-4E/F—J52-P-8A engine, A-4M—J52-P-408 engine
Thrust: A-4B/C—7,700 pounds, A-4E/F—9,300 pounds, A-4M—11,200 pounds
Dimensions: wingspan 27 feet 6 inches, length A-4A/B/C—38 feet 5 inches, A-4E/F/M—41 feet 4 inches; height 15 feet
Speed: cruise—410-433 knots, maximum—548-578 knots
Ceiling: 40,450 feet
Range: 1,200 nautical miles with external tanks
Armament: two 20mm cannon, rockets, missiles, and bombs carried externally
Maximum takeoff weight: 24,500 pounds
Crew: one—pilot

Photographs: Pages 6-7, left; 20, being refueled by A-6; 73, foreground; 74-75, 82-83.

F-5

USAF designation: F-5E/F Tiger II
Nickname: F-5

The F-5E Tiger II aircraft is a single-seat, supersonic, tactical fighter designed for air-to-air combat with additional air-to-surface capability. The F-5F Tiger II is a tandem-seat version of the E model, used in combat or operational training.

The U.S. Air Force and U.S. Navy use the F-5E as a realistic adversary in air combat training. "Aggressor squadrons" are equipped with F-5Es that closely resemble the MiG-21 in size and performance, and are painted in patterns typical of potential enemy aircraft. This enables U.S. tactical fighter pilots flying in mock air-to-air combat against F-5E pilots to develop the skills needed to defeat an enemy.

Tiger II electronics and equipment include full blind-flying instrumentation, an angle-of-attack system, and a central air-data computer. The radar system for air-to-air target searching and tracking has a range of 20 miles. Later versions have improved radar with angle track, 40-mile search capability, and automatic maneuvering flaps. Optional electronics include inertial navigation and instrument landing systems. The F-5E can be fitted with a reconnaissance nose for low/medium-altitude photoreconnaissance.

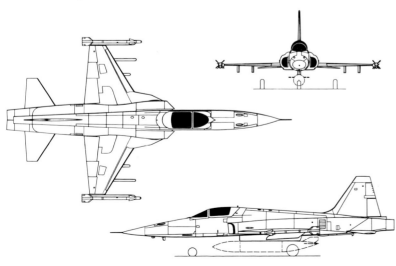

Primary function: tactical fighter
Prime contractor: Northrop Corporation
Power plant/manufacturer: two General Electric J85-GE-21 turbojet engines
Thrust: 5,000 pounds each engine with afterburner
Dimensions: wingspan 26 feet 8 inches, length F-5E—48 feet 2 inches, F-5F—51 feet 8 inches; height 13 feet 4 inches
Speed: at 36,000 feet, F-5E—Mach 1.6, F-5F—Mach 1.55
Ceiling: F-5E—51,800 feet, F-5F—50,800 feet
Range: more than 1,300 miles with external tanks
Armament: F-5E—two M-39 20mm cannons with 560 rounds of ammunition, F-5F—one M-39 20mm cannon with 140 rounds of ammunition; F-5E/F—two AIM-9 Sidewinder missiles on wing-tip launchers, variety of air-to-surface ordnance on five pylons
Maximum takeoff weight: 26,000 pounds
Crew: F-5E—one—pilot, F-5F—two—pilot, copilot

Photographs: Pages 6-7, right; 70-71, background; 72, 73, background; 76, inset view from F-5 cockpit; 76-77, 78, 80, being loaded with ordnance; 81.

A-6

USN designation: A-6E Intruder
Nickname: Intruder, BUFF

The A-6E is an all-weather, two-seat, carrier-based attack aircraft. It is equipped with a microminiaturized digital computer, a solid state weapons release system, and a single integrated track and search radar. The Target Recognition/Attack Multi-sensor (TRAM) version of the A-6E contains a Forward-Looking-Infra-Red (FLIR) system and a laser designator and receiver. It was introduced into the fleet in 1979.

The EA-6B Prowler, a four-seat derivation of the A-6, practices electronic warfare. It features a computer-controlled electronic surveillance and control system, and twelve high-power jamming transmitters in various frequency bands. The jamming transmitters are contained in pods mounted externally on five pylons. The capability

of the aircraft can be varied through the frequency spectrum by varying the mix of jamming transmitters.

Primary function: A-6E—destroy moving and fixed, sea and land targets, in all weather conditions, and during darkness; EA-6B—suppress and degrade enemy defense systems through jamming of enemy electronic signals
Prime contractor: Grumman Aerospace Corporation
Power plant/manufacturer: A-6E—two Pratt & Whitney J52-P8B turbojet engines, EA-6B—two Pratt & Whitney J52-P-408 engines
Thrust: A-6E—9,300 pounds each engine, EA-6B—11,000 pounds each engine
Dimensions: A-6E/EA-6B—wingspan 53 feet, length A-6E—54 feet 8 inches, EA-6B—59 feet 8 inches; height A-6E—15 feet 6 inches, EA-6B—16 feet 3 inches
Speed: A-6E—563 knots, EA-6B—520 knots at sea level with six pods
Range: 1,920 miles
Ceiling: A-6E—40,600 feet, EA-6B—34,400 feet
Armament: 15,000 pounds of bombs, rockets, nuclear weapons, and air-to-surface missiles
Maximum takeoff weight: A-6E—58,600 pounds, EA-6B—60,400 pounds
Crew: A-6E—two—pilot, bombardier/navigator; EA-6B—four—pilot, navigator, two electronic countermeasures officers

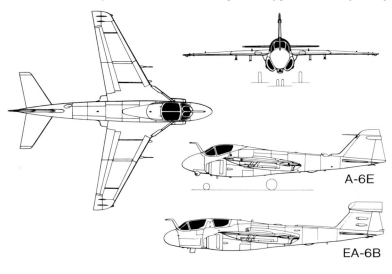

A-6E

EA-6B

Photographs: Pages 20, A-6 refueling A-4; 34, A-6 foreground, EA-6B background and launching; 40-41, A-6; 46, A-6 middle, EA-6B background; 84-85, A-6 refueling F-14; 118, A-6s and EA-6B foreground; 127, A-6s and EA-6B background.

A-3

USN designation: A-3 Skywarrior
Nickname: Whale

Contracted for in 1949 as the XA3D-1, the Skywarrior was to serve as the Navy's carrier-based, long-range bomber, capable of delivering a nuclear weapon on targets far inland from its base at sea. When the A-3D entered the fleet in 1956, however, its design was adapted for a number of other purposes: photographic, electronic countermeasures (ECM), and training. As *Polaris* submarines assumed the Navy's portion of the strategic nuclear mission, these functions and others became the main Skywarrior mission in carrier operations.

Redesignated in the early '60s as the A-3 series, the existing versions of the A-3B were used for special mission support. In this role, the "Whales" supported Southeast Asian combat action of the next decade, as well as served Navy mission needs elsewhere in the world. Although scheduled to be phased out in the mid-'70s, the Skywarrior has outlasted its predicted lifespan.

Primary function: special mission support
Prime contractor: Douglas Aircraft Company
Power plant/manufacturer: A-3A—two Pratt & Whitney J57-P-6 turbojet engines, A-3B—two Pratt & Whitney J57-P-10 turbojet engines
Thrust: A-3A—11,000 pounds each engine, A-3B—10,500 pounds each engine
Dimensions: wingspan 72 feet 6 inches, length A-3A—74 feet 5 inches, A-3B—74 feet 9 inches; height 22 feet 8 inches
Speed: A-3A—540 knots, A-3B—558 knots
Ceiling: A-3A—39,000 feet, A-3B—39,100 feet
Range: A-3A—1,000 nautical miles, A-3B—1,200 nautical miles
Armament: A-3A—8,700 pounds of bombs, nuclear weapons; two 20mm cannon in tail; A-3B—12,800 pounds of bombs, mines, and nuclear weapons; two 20mm cannon in tail
Maximum takeoff weight: 82,000 pounds
Crew: three—pilot, copilot/bombardier, navigator/gunner

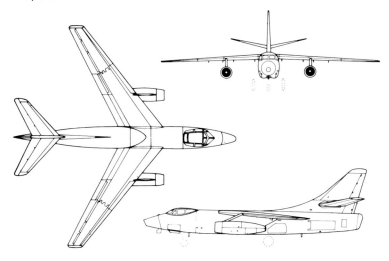

Photographs: Pages 32-33, 39, 86, F-14 cockpit view of A-3 refueling F-14; 87, F-14 cockpit view of A-3 refueling F-14; 88-89, A-3 refueling F-14; 108, 120, foreground; 124, foreground; 127, background.

E-2

USN designation: E-2C Hawkeye
Nickname: Hummer

The E-2C Hawkeye is the U.S. Navy's all-weather, carrier-based, tactical airborne warning and control system platform. Other missions include surface surveillance coordination, strike and interceptor control, search and rescue coordination, and communications relay. The E-2C is an integral component of the carrier air wing, configured with three primary sensors: radar, Identification Friend or Foe (IFF), and a passive detection system. These sensors are integrated with a general purpose computer which enables the E-2C to provide early warning, threat analyses, and control of counteraction against air and surface targets.

The E-2C radar system can maintain more than 600 tracks over land and water and can detect airborne targets anywhere within a three million cubic mile surveillance envelope. For example, an E-2C flying over New York can track all air traffic in the congested Boston-to-Washington air corridor.

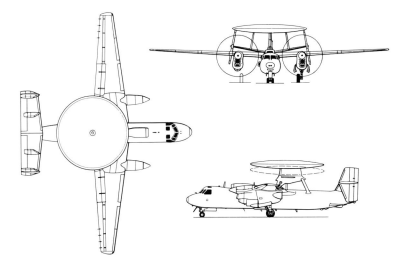

Primary function: all-weather airborne early warning, command, and control functions for the carrier battle group
Prime contractor: Grumman Aerospace Corporation
Power plant/manufacturer: two Allison T-56-A422 turboprop engines
Horsepower: 4,591 each engine
Dimensions: wingspan 80 feet 8 inches, length 57 feet 6 inches, height 18 feet 3 inches
Speed: cruise 270 knots
Ceiling: 30,800 feet
Maximum takeoff weight: 52,500 pounds
Crew: five or six—pilot, copilot, combat information center operator, weapons operator, air control operator, radar operator

Photographs: Pages 31, background; 34, background; 55, 103, background; 109, 118, background.

S-3

USN designation: S-3A Viking
Nickname: Hoover

The S-3A is a high-wing, high-subsonic, all-weather, long-range, high-endurance jet aircraft. It locates and destroys conventional as well as high-speed, deep-submergence, quiet-running submarines. With a large fuel capacity, it can range far to prosecute a contact or assist in targeting a surface contact.

The S-3A offers complete deck-level servicing accessibility, simplifying its shipboard maintenance through computerized fault-finding equipment, built-in test equipment (BITE), and versatile avionic shop test (VAST).

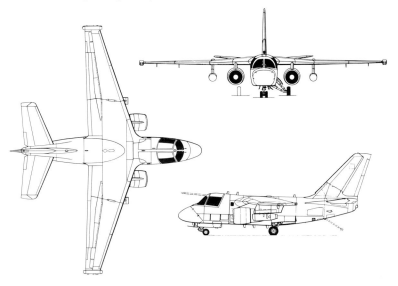

Primary function: seek and destroy enemy submarines, surface surveillance, subsurface attack
Prime contractor: Lockheed California
Power plant/manufacturer: two General Electric TF-34-GE-400 engines
Thrust: 9,275 pounds each engine
Dimensions: wingspan 68 feet 8 inches, length 53 feet 3 inches, height 22 feet 8 inches
Speed: 450 knots
Ceiling: 40,000 feet; service 10,670 feet
Range: combat over 2,000 nautical miles; ferry over 3,000 nautical miles
Armament: four MK-46 torpedoes, depth bombs, conventional bombs, harpoon missile, rockets, mines
Maximum takeoff weight: 52,500 pounds
Crew: four—pilot, copilot, tactical coordinator, accoustic sensor operator

Photographs: Pages 46, background; 104-105, US-3; 111, viewed from PLAT; 118, background; 127, foreground.

SH-3

USN designation: SH-3H Sea King
Nickname: None

The SH-3H is a twin-engine, all-weather, ship-based, antisubmarine helicopter. Equipment includes variable-depth sonar, sonobuoys (sonar devices that detect submerged submarines and relay information by radio), data link, chaff (foil strips dropped to confuse enemy radar systems), and a tactical navigation system.

The Sea King also provides logistic support and search and rescue capability when deployed aboard an aircraft carrier. The SH-3H accommodates 31 paratroopers in its troop lift role, 15 stretchers and a medical attendant in its casualty evacuation configuration, and 25 survivors in its search and rescue role.

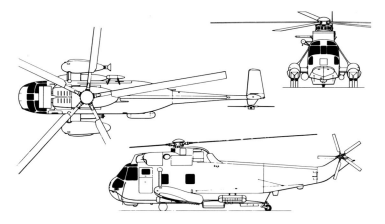

Primary function: detect, classify, track, and destroy enemy submarines
Prime contractor: Sikorsky Aircraft Division of United Technologies Corporation
Power plant/manufacturer: two General Electric T58-GE-10 turboshaft engines
Horsepower: 1,400 each engine
Dimensions: width 62 feet, length 72 feet 8 inches (maximum), height 15 feet 10 inches (maximum)
Speed: 144 knots
Ceiling: 10,800 feet
Range: 639 nautical miles; with 31 paratroops, 314 nautical miles
Maximum takeoff weight: 21,000 pounds
Crew: four—pilot, copilot, two sonar operators

Photographs: Pages 134, 135.

H-46

USN designation: H-46 Sea Knight
Nickname: None

Readily identified among Navy and Marine Corps helicopters are the H-46 series Sea Knights. Tandem rotors set them apart from the single-rotor design of other Navy/Marine helicopters. Special features of the early HRB-1 models included power-operated blade folding, integral cargo handling provisions, a rear-loading ramp that could be left open in flight, personnel recovery and rescue equipment, and provisions for hoisting 10,000 pounds externally. These features marked a significant step forward in helicopter capability.

Continued production brought modifications to improve the H-46. With service in Southeast Asia came installation of guns and armor. Increased weight and speed requirements were met by more powerful T-58-GE-16 engines. Cambered ("droop snoot") rotor blades were also added.

The early A models now serve as search and rescue HH-46As. CH-46s equip Marine reserve squadrons, and conversion of earlier aircraft to the CH-46E version is under way, with fiberglass blades slated to join other improvements.

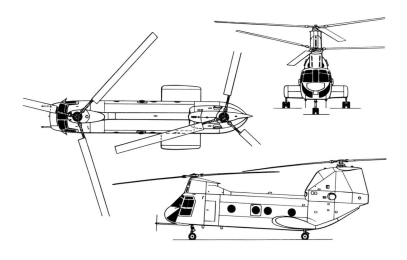

Primary function: transport
Prime contractor: Boeing/Vertol
Power plant/manufacturer: HH-46A—General Electric T-58-GE-8B engines, CH-46D/F—T-58-GE-10 engines, CH-46E—T-58-GE-16 engines
Horsepower: HH-46A—1,250 each engine; CH-46D/F—1,400 each engine; CH-46E—1,800 each engine
Dimensions: rotor diameter 50 feet, length (over rotors) 83 feet 4 inches, height 17 feet
Speed: 131 knots
Ceiling: service 12,800 feet, hover 7,300 feet
Range: 210 nautical miles
Maximum takeoff weight: 17-25 troops, 4,000 pounds of cargo
Crew: four—pilot, copilot, two air crewmen

Photographs: Pages 130-131, 132, 133.

CV-63

USN designation: CV-63 *Kitty Hawk*
Nickname: The Hawk

The *Kitty Hawk* was laid down by the New York Shipbuilding Corporation of Camden, New Jersey on December 27, 1956. It was launched May 21, 1960.

On June 6, 1963, President John F. Kennedy, with top civilian and military leaders, boarded *Kitty Hawk* to witness a carrier task force weapons demonstration off the California coast. *Kitty Hawk* was awarded the Navy Unit Commendation for exceptionally meritorious service from 1965 to 1966 while participating in combat operations against guerrilla forces in the Republic of Vietnam. From Yankee Station, *Kitty Hawk* flew around-the-clock missions over North Vietnam.

Kitty Hawk's designation was changed from CVA (attack aircraft carrier) to CV (multi-purpose) in April 1973, with the addition of A/S command centers, S-3A Vikings, and SH-3H helicopters. *Kitty Hawk* is scheduled to participate in the Service Life Extension Program (SLEP) from July 1987 to November 1989.

Primary function: multi-purpose aircraft carrier
Prime contractor: New York Shipbuilding Corporation
Displacement: 80,000 tons
Draught: 40 feet
Length: 1,069 feet
Beam: 129 feet 4 inches
Width: 273 feet
Flight deck area: 4.1 acres
Catapults: four steam
Main engines: four Westinghouse geared turbines
Horsepower: 280,000+
Boilers: eight Foster-Wheeler
Speed: 35 knots
Complement: 5,300 with air wing
Aircraft: approximately 85

CV-61

USN designation: CV-61 *Ranger*
Nickname: Top Gun of the Pacific Fleet

The *Ranger* was laid down by the Newport News Shipbuilding and Dry Dock Company on August 2, 1954, and was launched September 29, 1956. It is the eighth U.S. Navy ship to bear the name *Ranger.*

Ranger was called into combat on August 5, 1964, on her fifth deployment. Over the next ten years during the Vietnam War, she was engaged in armed conflict seven different times in Southeast Asia. In 1976, *Ranger* deployed to the Western Pacific to patrol peacetime shipping lanes. In 1979, she took her last cruise carrying F-4 jets. During the American hostage crisis in Iran, *Ranger* was deployed in the Persian Gulf for 130 days, awaiting the hostages' release.

Ranger is scheduled to participate in the Service Life Extension Program (SLEP) from January 1992 to May 1994.

Primary function: multipurpose aircraft carrier
Prime contractor: Newport News Shipbuilding and Dry Dock Company
Displacement: 80,000 tons
Draught: 37 feet
Length: 1,071 feet
Beam: 129 feet 5 inches
Width: 270 feet
Catapults: four steam
Main engines: four Westinghouse geared turbines
Horsepower: 280,000
Boilers: eight Babcock and Wilcox
Speed: 34 knots
Complement: 5,180 with air wing
Aircraft: approximately 80

Additional photographs of Russian aircraft: Pages 92, May; 94-95, Badger; 96, Bear; 97, Bear detail; 98, Badger flying over Russian ship; 99, Bears.

You may wonder how I made the photographs for this book. I shot more than five-hundred rolls of color slide film rated from ISO 25 to 1600. The majority of images were captured on Kodachrome 64 and Fujichrome 100. I used three motor-driven Nikon F-3s with Nikkor lenses from 16mm to 400mm. The equipment took quite a beating in the map case of my F-14 during carrier takeoffs and landings. I took at least one camera with me on every sortie. Even in the high G/high altitude environment, no modifications or special lubricants were necessary. Lens filters for special effects were never used, not even a U.V. or skylight. This cost me a couple of lenses, but shooting through the curved, scratched, Plexiglas canopy was all the extraneous material I wanted between my subject and the film. That way, I got the sharpest possible picture, and you see ex**actly what** I saw.

—*C.J. Heatley III*